United States
Department of
Agriculture

Forest Service

FS-977

May 2011

Watershed Condition Framework

A Framework for Assessing and Tracking Changes to Watershed Condition

"Restoration, for me, means managing forest lands first and foremost to protect our water resources while making our forests far more resilient to climate change. In many of our forests, restoration will also include efforts to improve or decommission roads, to replace and improve culverts, and to rehabilitate streams and wetlands. Restoration will also mean the rehabilitation of declining ecosystems."

Tom Vilsack
Secretary, U.S. Department of Agriculture
August 14, 2009

Cover photo: *Bridger Wilderness in Wyoming by Andrea Davidson.*

Contributors

Watershed Condition Advisory Team Members (October 2010)

John Potyondy	Washington Office (WO), Watershed, Fish, Wildlife, Air and Rare Plants (WFWARP), Stream Systems Technology Center
Ted Geier	Eastern Region (R-9), Regional Office, Regional Hydrologist
Penny Luehring	WO, WFWARP, Watershed Improvement Program Leader
Mark Hudy	WO, WFWARP, Fish and Aquatic Ecology Unit (FAEU)
Brett Roper	WO, WFWARP, FAEU
Ron Dunlap	WO, WFWARP, Assistant Director, Watershed, Fish, and Air (retired)
Tom Doane	Eastern Region, Deputy Director, Air, Water, Lands, Soils, Minerals and Environmental Engineering/Services
Greg Kujawa	WO, Forest Management
Paul T. Anderson	WO, Engineering
Jaelith Hall-Rivera	WO, Fire and Aviation Management
Jim Keys	WO, Ecosystem Management Coordination
Michael Ielmini	WO, Invasive Species Program
Ann Acheson	WO, WFWARP Air Program
Ray Thompson	WO, Program and Budget
Bob Davis	Southwestern Region (R-3), Regional Director's Representative
Sharon Friedman	Rocky Mountain Region (R-2), Strategic Planning Director
Karl Dalla Rosa	WO, State and Private Forestry (Forest Stewardship Program)
Thomas Brown	Rocky Mountain Research Station

Executive Summary

The Watershed Condition Framework (WCF) is a comprehensive approach for proactively implementing integrated restoration on priority watersheds on national forests and grasslands.

The WCF proposes to improve the way the Forest Service approaches watershed restoration by targeting the implementation of integrated suites of activities in those watersheds that have been identified as priorities for restoration. The WCF also establishes a nationally consistent reconnaissance-level approach for classifying watershed condition, using a comprehensive set of 12 indicators that are surrogate variables representing the underlying ecological, hydrological, and geomorphic functions and processes that affect watershed condition. Primary emphasis is on aquatic and terrestrial processes and conditions that Forest Service management activities can influence. The approach is designed to foster integrated ecosystem-based

watershed assessments; target programs of work in watersheds that have been identified for restoration; enhance communication and coordination with external agencies and partners; and improve national-scale reporting and monitoring of program accomplishments. The WCF provides the Forest Service with an outcome-based performance measure for documenting improvement to watershed condition at forest, regional, and national scales.

Why a Watershed Approach?

Watersheds are universal, well-defined areas that provide a common basis for discussion of water-related resources and landscapes.

Contents

Introduction

The U.S. Department of Agriculture (USDA) *Strategic Plan for FY 2010–2015* targets the restoration of watershed and forest health as a core management objective of the national forests and grasslands. To achieve this goal, the Forest Service, an agency of USDA, is directed to restore degraded watersheds by strategically focusing investments in watershed improvement projects and conservation practices at the landscape and watershed scales. The Watershed Condition Framework (WCF) is a comprehensive approach for classifying watershed condition, proactively implementing integrated restoration in priority watersheds on national forests and grasslands, and tracking and monitoring outcome-based program accomplishments for performance accountability.

In a 2006 review of the Forest Service Watershed Program, the Office of Management and Budget (OMB) concluded that the agency lacked a nationally consistent approach to prioritizing watersheds for improvement (OMB 2006). The OMB also noted that current Forest Service direction for tracking watershed condition class (FSM 2521) was vague, open to varied interpretation, and insufficient to consistently evaluate watershed condition or track how the condition changes over time. To address these issues, the Forest Service formed a National Watershed Condition Team and tasked it with developing a consistent, science-based approach to classify the condition of all National Forest System (NFS) watersheds and to develop outcome-based performance measures for watershed restoration.

The watershed condition policy goal of the Forest Service is "to protect National Forest System watersheds by implementing practices designed to maintain or improve watershed condition, which is the foundation for sustaining ecosystems and the production of renewable natural resources, values, and benefits" (FSM 2520). Secretary of Agriculture Tom Vilsack reemphasized this policy in his "Vision for the Forest Service," when he stated that restoring watershed and forest health would be the primary management objective of the Forest Service (USDA 2010). To help implement this new policy emphasis, the Forest Service developed the WCF.

The WCF provides a consistent way to evaluate watershed condition at both the national and forest levels. Watershed condition assessments by individual national forests are critical because local national forest staffs are the closest to the ground and best understand existing conditions. The WCF consists of reconnaissance-level assessments by individual national forests, implementation of integrated improvement activities within priority watersheds, validation and monitoring of watershed condition class changes, and aggregation of program performance data for national reporting.

The Goals of Watershed Restoration

The watershed condition goal of the Forest Service is "to protect National Forest System watersheds by implementing practices designed to maintain or improve watershed condition" (FSM 2520.2). The WCF provides a means to achieve this goal by—

- Establishing a systematic process for determining watershed condition class that all national forests can apply consistently.

- Fostering integrated ecosystem-based approaches for managing watersheds and aquatic resources.

- Strengthening the effectiveness of the Forest Service to maintain and restore the productivity and resilience of watersheds and their associated aquatic systems on NFS lands.

- Improving the internal dialog among disciplines to focus and integrate programs of work to efficiently maintain and restore watersheds and aquatic ecosystems.

- Enabling a coordinated and priority-based approach for allocating resources to restore watersheds.

- Enhancing coordination with external agencies and partners in watershed management and aquatic species recovery efforts.

- Improving national-scale reporting of watershed condition.

Defining Watershed Condition

Watershed condition is the state of the physical and biological characteristics and processes within a watershed that affect the soil and hydrologic functions supporting aquatic ecosystems. Watershed condition reflects a range of variability from natural pristine (functioning properly) to degraded (severely altered state or impaired). Watersheds that are functioning properly have terrestrial, riparian, and aquatic ecosystems that capture, store, and release water, sediment, wood, and nutrients within their range of natural variability for these processes. When watersheds are functioning properly, they create and sustain functional terrestrial, riparian, aquatic, and wetland habitats that are capable of supporting diverse populations of native aquatic- and riparian-dependent species. In general, the greater the departure from the natural pristine state, the more impaired the watershed condition is likely to be. Watersheds that are functioning properly are commonly referred to as healthy watersheds.

Watersheds that are functioning properly have five important characteristics (Williams et al. 1997):

1. They provide for high biotic integrity, which includes habitats that support adaptive animal and plant communities that reflect natural processes.

2. They are resilient and recover rapidly from natural and human disturbances.

3. They exhibit a high degree of connectivity longitudinally along the stream, laterally across the floodplain and valley bottom, and vertically between surface and subsurface flows.

4. They provide important ecosystem services, such as high-quality water, the recharge of streams and aquifers, the maintenance of riparian communities, and the moderation of climate variability and change.

5. They maintain long-term soil productivity.

Watershed condition classification is the process of describing watershed condition in terms of discrete categories (or classes) that reflect the level of watershed health or integrity. In the context of this framework, watershed health and integrity are conceptually the same (Regier 1993): watersheds with high integrity are in an unimpaired condition in which ecosystems show little or no influence from human actions (Lackey 2001).

The Forest Service Manual (FSM) uses three classes to describe watershed condition (USDA Forest Service 2004a, FSM 2521.1):

> Class 1 watersheds exhibit high geomorphic, hydrologic, and biotic integrity relative to their natural potential condition.

> Class 2 watersheds exhibit moderate geomorphic, hydrologic, and biotic integrity relative to their natural potential condition.

> Class 3 watersheds exhibit low geomorphic, hydrologic, and biotic integrity relative to their natural potential condition.

The FSM classification defines watershed condition in terms of "geomorphic, hydrologic and biotic integrity" relative to "potential natural condition." In this context, integrity relates directly to functionality. Geomorphic functionality or integrity can be defined in terms of attributes such as slope stability, soil erosion, channel morphology, and other upslope, riparian, and aquatic habitat characteristics. Hydrologic functionality or integrity relates primarily to flow, sediment, and water-quality attributes. Biological functionality or integrity is defined by the characteristics that influence the diversity and abundance of aquatic species, terrestrial vegetation, and soil productivity. In each case, integrity is evaluated in the context of the natural disturbance regime, geoclimatic setting, and other important factors within the context of a watershed. The definition encompasses both aquatic and terrestrial components, because water quality and aquatic habitat are inseparably related to the integrity and, therefore, the functionality of upland and riparian areas within a watershed.

The three watershed condition classes are directly related to the degree or level of watershed functionality or integrity:

Class 1 = Functioning Properly.

Class 2 = Functioning at Risk.

Class 3 = Impaired Function.

In this framework, we characterize a watershed in good condition as one that is functioning in a manner similar to natural wildland conditions (Karr and Chu 1999, Lackey 2001). This characterization should not be interpreted to mean that managed watersheds cannot be in good condition. A watershed is considered to be functioning properly if the physical attributes are appropriate to maintain or improve biological integrity. This consideration implies that a Class 1 watershed in properly functioning condition has minimal undesirable human impact on natural, physical, or biological processes and is resilient and able to recover to the desired condition when or if disturbed by large natural disturbances or land management activities (Yount and Neimi 1990). By contrast, a Class 3 watershed has impaired function because some physical, hydrological, or biological threshold has been exceeded. Substantial changes to the factors that caused the degraded state are commonly needed to set them on a trend or trajectory of improving conditions that sustain physical, hydrological, and biological integrity.

Defining specific classes for watershed condition is obviously subjective and, therefore, problematic for several reasons. First, watershed condition is not directly observable (Suter 1993). In nature, no distinct lines separate a watershed that is functioning properly from impaired condition, and every classification scheme is arbitrary to some extent. Second, watershed condition is a mental construct that has numerous definitions and interpretations in the scientific literature (Lackey 2001). Third, the attributes that reflect the state of a watershed are continually changing because of natural disturbances (e.g., wildfire, landslides, floods, insects, and disease), natural variability of ecological processes (e.g., flows and cycles of energy, nutrients, and water), climate variability and change, and human modifications.

Watershed-Scale Restoration

The most effective way to approach complex ecological issues is to consider them at the watershed level, where the fundamental connection among all components of the landscape is the network of streams that defines the watershed (Heller 2004, National Research Council 1999, Newbold 2002, Ogg and Keith 2002, Reid et al. 1996, Sedell et al. 2000, Smith et al. 2005, Williams et al. 1997). Watersheds are easily identified on maps and on the ground, and their boundaries do not change much over time (Reid et al. 1996). Watersheds are also readily recognized by local communities and resonate with members of the public as a logical way to address resource management issues.

Watersheds are integral parts of broader ecosystems and can be viewed and evaluated at a variety of spatial scales. Because watersheds are spatially located landscape features uniformly mapped for the entire United States at multiple scales, they are ideal for tracking accomplishments both in terms of outputs (acres treated on the ground) and outcomes (improvement in watershed condition class). To avoid double counting, we report accomplishments and outcomes by each watershed's unique hydrologic unit code (HUC). A watershed's condition class integrates the effect of all activities within a watershed; therefore, watersheds provide an ideal mechanism for interpreting the cumulative effect of a multitude of management actions on soil and hydrologic function. Finally, many hydrologic and aquatic restoration issues can be properly addressed only within the confines of watershed boundaries. Watersheds provide an excellent basis for developing restoration plans that can treat a multitude of resource problems in a structured, comprehensive manner.

Many terrestrial ecological restoration issues are poorly addressed, however, in a watershed context. Ecological restoration involves replacing lost or damaged biological elements (populations, species) and reestablishing ecological processes (dispersal, succession) at historical rates. Ecological restoration, because it deals with vegetation and wildlife species composition, structure, pattern, and diversity, may not affect soil and hydrologic function. Consequently, ecological restoration and condition are often best evaluated using ecological stratifications such as those depicted in the map Bailey's Ecoregions and Subregions of the United States, Puerto Rico, and the U.S. Virgin Islands (Bailey 1995), rather than watersheds.

The Six-Step Watershed Condition Framework

The scope of the WCF is broad and it encompasses multiple resource areas. The Forest Service Watershed Program, as defined by OMB and the Forest Service Strategic Plan, encompasses all Forest Service activities that contribute to improved watershed condition (OMB 2006, USDA Forest Service 2004b), including soil and water improvements, vegetation management, reforestation, range management, wildlife and fisheries improvements, road decommissioning, and other activities. Watershed restoration refers to activities that improve the conditions of watersheds, restore degraded habitats, and provide long-term protection to soils and aquatic and riparian resources. All management activities that influence watershed condition have a role to play in this context.

The WCF represents a paradigm shift in watershed restoration for the Forest Service (Bohn and Kershner 2002, Heller 2004, Sedell et al. 2000) in that it provides a framework to treat whole watersheds with an integrated set of watershed-scale restoration treatments (table 1). Working with entire watersheds makes it possible to reestablish the structure and function of an ecosystem to a close approximation of its condition before human disturbance (Williams et al. 1997). In the context of the WCF, watershed restoration is a comprehensive, long-term program to restore watershed health, riparian ecosystems, fish habitats, and soil productivity (Ziemer 1997).

The process is more strategic, better integrated, and more likely to contribute to long-term change in watershed conditions than current project-level improvement activities that may not be coordinated at the forest level. The WCF consists of an iterative process involving six steps (fig. 1).

The six steps of the WCF are—

Step A: Classify the condition of all 6th-level watersheds in the national forest by using existing data layers, local knowledge, and professional judgment.

Step B: Prioritize watersheds for restoration: establish a small set of priority watersheds for targeted improvement equivalent to a 5-year program of work.

Step C: Develop Watershed Restoration Action Plans that identify comprehensive project-level improvement activities.

Step D: Implement integrated suites of projects in priority watersheds.

Step E: Track restoration accomplishments for performance accountability.

Step F: Verify accomplishment of project activities and monitor improvement of watershed and stream conditions.

Table 1.—*Characteristics of the new paradigm proposed by this framework compared with the old paradigm for restoring aquatic- and riparian-dependent resources (Heller 2004).*

New Paradigm (Watershed Condition Framework)	Old Paradigm
1. The "best" watersheds are treated first. Highest priority treatments remove risk factors that may threaten the integrity of the watershed.	1. The "worst" watersheds are treated first. Highest priority is to create desired habitat conditions for stream segments/sites in the worst condition.
2. Efforts focus on a few priority watersheds.	2. Treatments tend to focus on stream segments or sites. They are scattered over several watersheds.
3. Watershed analysis precedes project work, identifies key processes, and prioritizes areas and associated treatment approaches that address "causes."	3. Analysis is generally limited to the project scale and to addressing site-scale conditions. Treatments address "symptoms."
4. A wide range of treatments are generally integrated at a watershed scale and sequenced based on an overall work plan.	4. A narrow range of treatments usually focuses on individual sites. They are not integrated at the watershed scale.
5. Suites of essential projects are completed in a watershed before work emphasis shifts to the next priority watershed.	5. Highest priority work is completed on individual areas or sites located in a number different watersheds.
6. Partnerships are an essential part of restoration. Skills and resources are strongly leveraged.	6. Partnerships are limited in number and scope. Skills and resources are only somewhat leveraged.

Figure 1.—*Conceptual diagram of the six-step watershed condition framework process.*

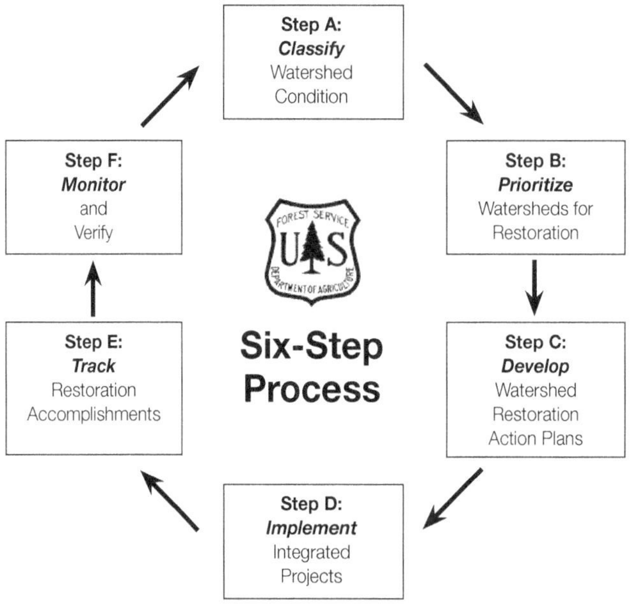

National forest units, with regional support, are primarily responsible for implementing the WCF. Forests must link local priorities with regional and national priorities, implement projects, and track costs and changes to watershed condition class. Regions provide valuable oversight to ensure program consistency. National leadership uses the assessment information gathered during the WCF process to establish national priorities, evaluate Forest Service program performance, and communicate results to interested stakeholders and customers.

Roles and Responsibilities

The following roles and responsibilities pertain to Watershed Condition Assessment (FSM 2521) and Watershed Improvement (FSM 2522).

The Director of the Watershed, Fish, Wildlife, Air, and Rare Plants Program Staff, Washington Office (WO), has the responsibility to—

- Consult and coordinate with other Federal agencies to develop approaches and guidance for watershed delineation, watershed assessment, and classification of watershed condition.

- Develop criteria and standards for classifying watershed condition for the Government Performance and Results Act (GPRA) assessment, forest plans, and program development.

- Develop criteria for determining and displaying watershed condition trends for the GPRA assessment, forest plans, and program development.

- Use the results of watershed condition analyses for the GPRA assessment and as a basis for defining needs and opportunities in the program alternatives.

- Develop policy and program direction and assign targets for the watershed improvement program.

Regional foresters have the responsibility to—

- Develop guidelines and procedures, based on national criteria and standards, for establishing priorities for assessing and monitoring watershed conditions and trends. Ensure that assessment and monitoring data are available in a corporate database. Provide technical and administrative oversight of the forest classification process.

- Determine how watershed condition will be integrated in regional, forest, and project planning processes.

- Work with States, tribes, and other interested parties to identify watersheds as priorities for protection, management, and improvement.

- Use economic and environmental analyses to help identify opportunities for improving and maintaining watershed conditions.

- Establish regional priority guidelines for watershed improvement projects.

- Establish and maintain a corporate database of watershed improvement needs.

- Provide training for personnel involved in watershed improvement planning, project implementation, maintenance, monitoring, and reviews.

Forest supervisors have the responsibility to—

- Assess (classify watershed condition) and monitor watershed conditions and trends and enter data into a corporate database.

- Work with States, tribes, local governments, and other interested parties to identify watersheds as priorities for protection and management and for improvement.

- Coordinate watershed priorities and resource management activities on NFS lands to attain forest plan goals and objectives for watershed condition.

- Cooperate with other agencies, groups, and individuals whose plans or proposals affect watershed conditions on NFS lands.

- Maintain a watershed improvement needs inventory in a corporate database.

- Identify priority watersheds for restoration; develop and approve prescriptions and plans for a forest watershed improvement program. Delegate the development of detailed prescriptions and plans to the district rangers when expertise is available at the district level.

- Ensure that funded watershed condition improvement projects are accomplished and that treatment measures are implemented as prescribed and approved.

Each of the six sequential steps of the WCF is discussed in greater detail in this framework. The intent of this framework is to provide sufficient guidance for consistent implementation of the WCF by national forests.

Step A: Classify Watershed Condition

Watershed classification will adhere to the following guidance:

- Forests will follow the classification direction in the *Forest Service Watershed Condition Technical Guide* (USDA Forest Service 2011).

- All national forests will classify 6th-level HUC watersheds into one of three Forest Service Watershed Condition Classes (FSM 2521.1): Class 1—Functioning Properly; Class 2—Functioning at Risk; Class 3—Functionally Impaired.

- An interdisciplinary team will classify watershed conditions. The classification process is office based and requires approximately 1 week for resource specialists to assemble necessary information and 1 week for the interdisciplinary team to classify all 6th-level watersheds.

- Classification is required for all 6th-level watersheds that contain any NFS lands.

- The classification will use the 12 core national indicators (fig. 2).

Figure 2.—*Core national watershed condition indicators and attributes.*

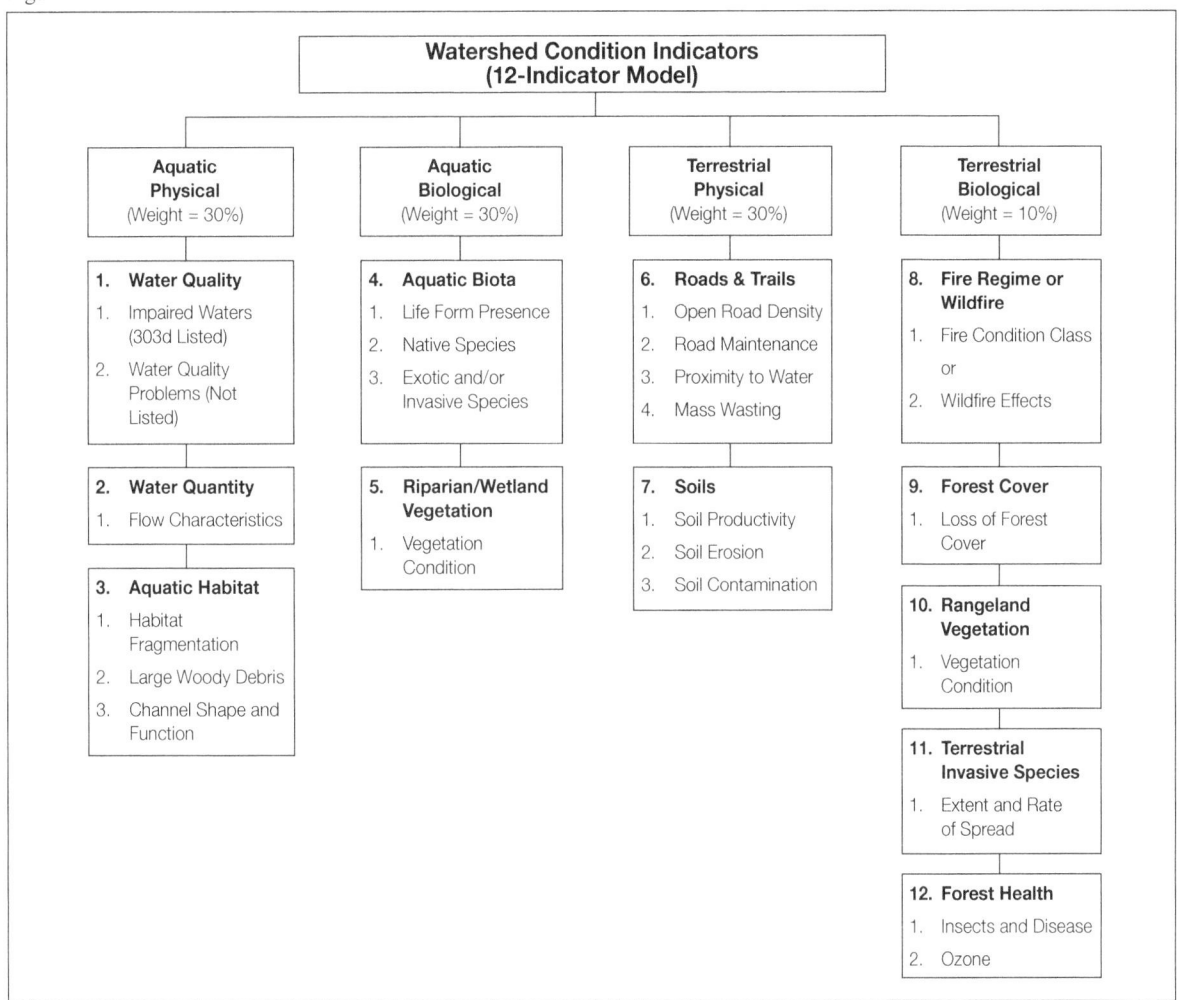

- Classification data will be stored in the corporate Watershed Classification and Assessment Tracking Tool (WCATT) and updated annually.

- The WO Watershed, Fish, Wildlife, Air, and Rare Plants Program Staff will have primary responsibility for national technical oversight, and members of the Watershed Condition Advisory Team will assist them. This oversight includes managing the change process, ensuring consistency among regions, and providing national Geographic Information System data products and software for use in classification.

- The regional offices will oversee the forest classification processes. This oversight includes ensuring consistency among the forests in the region, approving the use of forest modifications to attributes and the override option, coordinating classification with adjoining regions and national forests, and consulting with the WO when significant modifications are approved.

Step B: Prioritize Watersheds for Restoration

Under the WCF, the task of identifying watersheds for restoration is left to the discretion of national forests within the broad framework of national direction, regional emphasis, forest plan direction, resource value, costs, local issues, needs, the amount of NFS lands, and opportunities. Selecting watersheds for restoration is a distinct process that takes place after watershed classification (Step A) has been completed. The amount of NFS lands and the ability to effect a change in watershed condition are important considerations in the priority-setting process.

The Forest Service does not have the capability to improve the condition of every watershed. The ability to improve watershed condition is contingent on many factors, including the percent of the Forest Service's ownership, ownership location and pattern, source and degree of disturbances, existing partnerships, and other factors. One of the most important factors is the size of the watershed; the smaller the watershed, the more likely it will be to show change to watershed conditions. Sixth-level HUC watersheds[1] were chosen specifically as the base for tracking improvement to watershed condition because they are, on average, 10,000 to 40,000 acres in size. Consequently, 6th-level watersheds are the scale used for priority watersheds.

Forests should identify an appropriate number of watersheds for maintenance or improvement that correspond to a reasonable and achievable program of work over the next 5 years within current budget levels. Priority watersheds are the designated watersheds where restoration activities will concentrate on the explicit goal of maintaining or improving watershed condition. The number of priority watersheds will vary by national forest but is expected to range from one to five, given current funding levels.

The identification of watersheds will use an interdisciplinary team process that includes representatives from soil, water, range, wildlife and fish, engineering, vegetation, planning, fuels, and others as appropriate. The forest supervisor needs to approve the priority watershed. For cases in which one or more forests share watersheds, the affected forests and regions will need to work together to ensure that the selection of watersheds is coordinated. The participation of partners (local, State, tribal, other Federal agencies, and interest groups) in the watershed prioritization process is both expected and highly encouraged.

In summary, the prioritization of watersheds is a forest-based interdisciplinary process with the goal of aligning watershed restoration work with both internal and external priorities. The identification of priority watersheds is based on the following:

- Agency watershed restoration policies and priorities that have been established at other scales, including national- and regional-scale restoration strategies.

- The importance of water and watershed resources (resource value), the urgency of management action to address conditions and threats, and economic considerations.

- Alignment with other Forest Service strategic objectives and priorities.

- Alignment with the strategies and priorities of other Federal and State agencies, tribes, community and collaborative efforts, nongovernmental conservation organizations, and public desires.

Forest Service Policy, Direction, and Guidance

All watershed prioritization occurs within the context of national-, regional-, and forest-level decisionmaking. The following sections address direction for watershed condition for each organizational level.

National Direction

National direction for watershed condition is contained in the *USDA Forest Service Strategic Plan for FY 2007–2012* (USDA Forest Service 2007). Goal 1 is to "Restore, sustain, and enhance the Nation's forests and grasslands" (USDA Forest Service 2007). Objective 1.5 is to "Restore and maintain healthy watersheds and diverse habitats" (USDA Forest Service 2007).

---

[1] In the context of WCF, the terms *watershed* and *hydrologic unit* are used synonymously. Hydrologic units, however, are truly synonymous only with the classic watershed definition when their boundaries include all the source area contributing surface water to a single defined outlet point. For the intended uses of the WCF, this distinction is relatively unimportant. Also, strictly speaking, 6th-level HUCs are called *subwatersheds*. We use the term watershed to include a wide range of watershed sizes.

National policy is to use watershed conditions to help prioritize watersheds and consider resource factors, risks, values and benefits, economics, social factors, and partnership opportunities when setting priorities (FSM 2521.11b). Priorities for improving watershed condition are assigned in order of decreasing importance as follows (FSM 2522.03):

- Those posing menace to life or property because of flood threats or possible mud or debris flows.

- Those needing action to maintain water quality or achieve other forest plan goals and objectives.

- Those not meeting, or facing an imminent threat of not meeting, water quality requirements of the forest plan.

Annual Vegetation and Watershed Program direction priorities are to maintain high-value watersheds and to improve degraded watersheds. Emphasis is on the following (USDA Forest Service 2009):

- Maintaining watersheds that have important ecological values, such as those with designations of Outstanding Natural Resource Waters, Class A/Blue Ribbon fisheries, Class I Air sheds, Biodiversity Hotspots, etc.

- Improving impaired ecosystems, such as those with Clean Water Act § 303(d): listed waters, threatened or endangered species, poor air quality, invasive species, or degraded vegetation conditions and those where improvement or restoration activities are necessary to meet regulatory requirements or meet desired condition objectives.

The FY 2011 Forest Service Program Direction emphasizes concentrating restoration activities in a few select locations to show meaningful improvement to watershed condition.

> "The overarching priority for restoration is on the implementation of integrated ecosystem restoration projects on priority [targeted] watersheds at the hydrologic unit code (HUC) 6 scale, with the goal of improving the targeted watershed's condition class. Priority should be given to implementing integrated ecosystem restoration projects that are collaborative and part of an all-land, large-scale conservation strategy. Restoration efforts are to focus on repairing impairments to the natural diversity and ecological dynamics of National Forest System (NFS) lands; providing ecosystem services that are important to the public including clean and abundant water, renewable energy from biomass, restored wildlife

and fish habitat, forest products, and resilient forests and rangelands; and stabilizing and creating jobs" (1417–1418).

The intent of the national direction is to, first and foremost, protect high-value watersheds already in good condition, maintain the condition of watersheds to keep them from becoming threatened and, then, improve those in an impaired condition. Decisions to designate highly altered watersheds as priority watersheds need to be carefully considered because the Forest Service could invest large amounts of funding and resources trying to repair only a few, badly impaired watersheds that may never recover. Passive restoration, allowing natural processes to return to a watershed by stopping activities that cause degradation or prevent recovery, can be a cost-effective solution for some watersheds. Another way to maintain watershed conditions is to invest funding in maintenance activities, such as implementing best management practices, maintaining roads, managing range allotment, or conducting other activities to prevent further degradation (e.g., keep a Class 1 watershed from slipping into Class 2 condition). Although maintenance is important to protect watershed condition, the Forest Service currently has no mechanism for capturing this benefit in the performance accountability process. Implementing the National Best Management Practices Implementation and Effectiveness Monitoring Program is expected to provide the Forest Service with a partial mechanism for capturing the costs and benefits of actions taken to maintain watershed condition.

Regional Direction

Each region has specific management direction and emphasis areas that pertain to forest management and watershed condition. Each national forest is advised to tier its priorities to regional guidance, as appropriate. The following examples from two regions demonstrate different approaches to watershed restoration.

The Pacific Northwest Region uses the following set of key principles to guide watershed restoration:

- Protect, restore, and enlarge refuge areas.

- Focus on effective treatments in priority areas.

- Implement activities restoring ecosystem processes and natural disturbance regimes.

- Learn through monitoring, researching, and adaptive management.

The focus of the Northern Region Integrated Restoration and Protection Strategy is to manage an integrated approach for the following:

- Restore and maintain high-value watersheds in properly functioning condition.

- Restore and maintain wildlife habitats, including restoration of more resilient vegetation conditions, where appropriate, to meet ecological and social goals.

- Protect people, structures, and community infrastructure (roads, bridges, and power corridors) in and associated with the wildland-urban interface.

Forest Plan Direction

Each national forest implements restoration direction from its land and resource management plan. Most forest plans include established priorities based on some combination of watershed condition derived from watershed analysis, values at risk, and the degree to which known impacts and threats could be feasibly and effectively addressed from technical, legal, political, social, and economic perspectives, including partnership opportunities.

Watershed restoration direction in many forest plans applies at a larger scale—the 5th-level HUC. In these cases, forests may wish to select all 6th-level watersheds within an important 5th-level watershed as their prioritized watersheds.

Resource Value

The following simple ranking approach (High, Moderate) is provided as an efficient way to estimate the relative resource value of each classified watershed. Forests may use more comprehensive approaches if they wish (e.g., Calkin et al. 2007). The rapid assessment proposed used here is simple, intending to rate watersheds in an efficient manner using available information. The assessment should take no more than 1 day, and the interdisciplinary team of each forest should tailor the assessment to the context of the local ecosystems and pertinent resource issues.

In this resource value assessment, we define resource value from the perspective of environmental and ecological value rather than from a commodity value viewpoint. Typically, watersheds with the highest resource values should receive the highest priority for protection or improvement.

The proposed assessment requires identifying the resource values associated with the special designations listed below. The forest interdisciplinary team rates each watershed.

Watersheds meeting at least one of the special designations are ranked High; the others are rated Moderate.

- Designated wilderness.

- Experimental watersheds and research natural areas.

- Designated municipal watersheds (source-water protection areas).

- Outstanding Resource Waters or other status to protect water quality or supplies.

- Designated protection area or habitat for aquatic threatened and endangered species (e.g., fish, amphibians, or mussels).

- Blue Ribbon Trout Streams or similar State or other designations.

- Wild and scenic rivers (designated or eligible study segments) or other unique recreational uses.

- Forest-specified resource value of a unique local characteristic.

Estimated Cost

A simple interval-scale ranking process is proposed to provide a coarse-scale estimate of the magnitude of costs and other investments that will be needed to improve the condition of individual watersheds. One can think of this process as a simple economic-feasibility ranking for preliminary planning purposes. The intent is to ensure that economics is considered in establishing priorities.

Forests need to recognize that this process will not be a precise estimate and should plan to spend no more than 1 day estimating cost categories. This lack of precision is because the activities that will need to be done to improve watershed conditions are only partially to poorly known at this time. Consequently, a coarse, qualitative assessment is appropriate.

For each watershed, estimate the total cost of all investments and National Environmental Policy Act (NEPA) consultation necessary to move the watershed to an improved condition class; consider watershed size, location, and the complexity and cost of anticipated activities and assign it one of the following five categories. This estimate will only be used to inform priority setting.

Cost Category 1	< $100,000
Cost Category 2	$100,000 to $1 million
Cost Category 3	$1 million to $5 million
Cost Category 4	$5 million to $15 million
Cost Category 5	> $15 million

Step C: Develop Watershed Restoration Action Plans

For priority watersheds, forests will develop a Watershed Restoration Action Plan that identifies specific projects necessary to improve watershed condition class.

A detailed field assessment is the basis for the action plan. The assessment should document specific problems affecting watershed and ecological conditions; identify appropriate projects that address these problems; propose an implementation schedule; and project sequencing, potential partners, funding sources, monitoring, and evaluation.

A typical Watershed Restoration Action Plan would include the following categories:

1. Executive Summary
   a. Watershed Name, HUC
   b. General Location
   c. Watershed Area
   d. General Physiography
   e. Land Use
   f. Key Problems
   g. Restoration Opportunities/Priorities

2. Watershed Characteristics and Conditions
   a. General Context/Overview
      (1) Climate
      (2) Hydrology
      (3) Geomorphology
      (4) Fisheries
      (5) Other Resources
   b. Watershed Conditions
      (1) Uplands/Hillslope Conditions
      (2) Riparian Conditions
      (3) Inchannel Habitat Conditions

3. Restoration Goals, Objectives, and Opportunities
   a. Goal Identification and Desired Condition
   b. Objectives, Existing and Post-Project Watershed Condition Class
   c. Opportunities
   d. Specific Project Activities (Essential Projects)

   e. Costs
   f. Timelines and Project Scheduling
   g. Partners

4. Restoration Project Monitoring and Evaluation

Acceptable watershed assessment methods must be used to analyze watershed condition and make recommendations for needed improvements. Examples of accepted methods include the following: Ecosystem Analysis at the Watershed Scale (Regional Ecosystem Office 1995), Hydrologic Condition Analysis (McCammon et al. 1998), Total Maximum Daily Load assessments, and Watershed Improvement Needs inventories. Forests may use other methods (Bohn and Kershner 2002, Rosgen 2006), provided the assessment method has sufficient information about watershed function and processes to determine specific problems and current and desired watershed conditions, and if it provides information that can be used to identify restoration activities.

The field-based watershed condition assessment will be documented in a Watershed Restoration Action Plan that synthesizes problems, actions, and timelines. Identifying essential projects is a primary goal.

Essential Projects and Approval Process

Essential projects are a discreet group of conservation actions and treatments that are implemented as an integrated suite of on-the-ground management activities focused primarily on restoring watershed health and thereby improving watershed condition class. They may include practices such as soil and water improvement, fisheries and aquatic resource habitat improvement, aquatic organism passage improvement, road decommissioning, road maintenance, upslope surface erosion control, reforestation, hazardous fuel reduction, restoring fire-adapted ecosystems, obtaining instream flows, negotiating flow regime changes below reservoirs, or other activities that when implemented, sustain or improve a watershed's condition class.

Essential projects either directly correct a problem (e.g., restore an abandoned mine) or substantially reduce risk to soil, hydrologic, or riparian function (e.g., invasive weed treatment, hazardous fuels reduction, or off-highway vehicle damage prevention). Essential projects may be individual projects or a group of projects that cumulatively require work or action to maintain or improve watershed condition class. A watershed will generally require a suite of essential projects to move it to a better condition class (e.g., decommission 5 roads, upgrade 15 culverts, change a grazing system, remove 3 check dams, remove hazardous fuels from 30 acres of riparian area, and restore native riparian vegetation).

Essential projects in a priority watershed target multiple resource issues and are funded from many fund codes. Federal, State, or other partners interested in watershed restoration may also finance essential projects.

Although emphasis is on on-the-ground work, essential projects can also include planning aspects associated with air quality regulatory activities that result in improved watershed condition.

Because air quality and watershed condition are directly linked, forests have the ability to identify "active participation in the air regulatory process" as an essential project for those watersheds affected by air pollution. Similar to other essential projects, credit will be taken when projects are completed, rather than when positive effects fully manifest themselves.

An interdisciplinary team identifies essential projects, and then the appropriate line officer reviews and considers the project recommendations put forward by the interdisciplinary team. The watershed is considered to have moved to an improved condition class and reported as such when all of the essential projects necessary to move a watershed to an improved class and identified in a Watershed Restoration Action Plan are completed.

Step D: Implement Integrated Projects

Treating whole watersheds with an integrated set of watershed-scale restoration treatments is no trivial matter. On average, a complex integrated watershed restoration process, from watershed analysis to action plan completion, may take 5 to 6 years, or longer.

The planning phase alone may take 3 years or more. This phase includes meeting NEPA requirements to assess the potential environmental consequences of the watershed improvement project, evaluation of alternatives, and opportunity for public review and comment. Significant time may be needed for fieldwork and analysis to support the Watershed Restoration Action Plan followed by project design for specific treatments. These planning tasks may cost hundreds of thousands of dollars for a typical project.

To be truly effective, most watershed-based restoration efforts require the involvement of partners. Collaboration has many benefits, but it may be time-consuming to obtain the support of interested parties.

Once planning is completed, because of the numerous projects typically included in a Watershed Restoration Action Plan, many restoration projects can be expected to have a 3-year or longer implementation phase. A watershed is considered to have moved to an improved condition class and is reported as such when all of the essential projects identified in a Watershed Restoration Action Plan are completed.

Step E: Track Restoration Accomplishments

For tracking restoration accomplishments, changes to watershed condition will most likely result from planned, active restoration in priority watersheds. A change in watershed condition class may, however, occur for a variety of other reasons, and change may occur in prioritized or other watersheds, for example, because of management actions, as the result of natural disturbances, or even as a consequence of climate change. Other factors that could cause a change to watershed conditions unrelated to priority watersheds might include a State water-quality agency declaring that a listed water body is now in compliance with State water-quality standards, a negotiated change to the flow regime of a reservoir, wildfires, natural disasters, or other watershed altering activities. The direction of change to a watershed's condition could be positive or negative and may affect priority or other watersheds. This complexity introduces a level of uncertainty into the watershed condition class tracking process. Therefore, watershed condition class changes need to be care-fully interpreted to understand the causes of those changes. The working assumption is that most of the changes reflected in performance accountability will be driven by actions in priority watersheds.

The WCATT tracks watershed condition class for all 6th-level HUC watersheds. WCATT is updated annually by forests concentrating on watersheds known to have experienced significant change. The condition class classification data (number of watersheds in each class) reported in WCATT will be automatically accessed and reported through the Performance Accountability System (PAS).

Essential projects, predetermined in a Watershed Restoration Action Plan, count toward changing watershed condition class upon their successful completion. Improvement to watershed condition is recorded upon project completion as a practical matter fully recognizing that actual improvement to watershed and stream condition may lag the completion of essential projects by years or decades. When they have completed all essential projects in a priority watershed, forests will remove the watershed from the priority list and replace it with another. A two- to three-person team of resource specialists, designated by the forest-level line officer, will evaluate watersheds where essential projects have been completed to certify the satisfactory completion of work in the priority watershed.

Performance Tracking

Restoration accomplishment will be reported in existing corporate performance accomplishment databases. Options under consideration include the Watershed Improvement Tracking (WIT) System; the Wildlife, Fish, and Rare Plant Management System (WFRP-MS); and the Performance Accountability System (PAS).

If selected as the repository of watershed accomplishments, these systems will need to be modified. Tracking costs and accomplishments and reporting improvement to watershed condition class will be a long-term endeavor, and existing budget structures based on single fiscal year expenditures and accomplishment reporting are ill suited for tracking multiyear projects. Refining the Forest Service budget and performance reporting systems will likely be necessary to track watershed scale restoration implemented under the WCF. The inclusion of geotagging features is highly effective for demonstrating restoration accomplishment.

Performance Measures

The Forest Service will need to track both outcome and outputs (acres treated). The primary outcome measure used to track accomplishments will be the number of watershed condition classes that have changed in a given year. Note that change may come from priority watersheds due to restoration actions or from nonpriority watersheds due to other factors.

The following performance measures will be used:

CLS-I-WTRSHD	Number of watersheds within condition class I.
CLS-II-WTRSHD	Number of watersheds within condition class II.
CLS-III-WTRSHD	Number of watersheds within condition class III.
WTRSHD-CLS-IMP-NUM	Number of watersheds moved to an improved condition class.

Step F: Verify and Monitor Watershed Condition Class

We propose a two-tiered approach to verify and monitor watershed conditions. Tier 1 emphasizes verifying for performance accountability. Tier 2 emphasizes monitoring linkages between watershed restoration treatments and the effect they have on aquatic habitat conditions.

Because of budget constraints, emphasis in the near term is on performance accountability (Tier 1). Over the long term, our goal is to develop a monitoring approach system that can link changes in watershed condition on the landscape to improvement to stream channel and aquatic habitat conditions (Tier 2). This long-term goal is consistent with the Chief's articulation in the FY 2011 Forest Service Budget Justification that the "Forest Service will establish a monitoring program so that in five years the Agency will be able to tune and support its risk-based approach to assessing and improving watershed condition" (Forest Service, 2010: 7–8).

Tier 1: Verifying for Performance Accountability

Tier 1 verification monitoring consists of reviewing watershed classification (Do watersheds appear to have been properly classified? Was the correct process followed in evaluating the extent to which prescribed restoration actions (essential projects) appear to have improved watershed condition compared with the indicators used for classification? Does it seem reasonable to conclude that the essential projects are of sufficient scope and magnitude to actually improve watershed condition class? Does the watershed now classify as being in an improved condition class?).

The fundamental assumption for performance accountability is that the completion of essential projects identified in the Watershed Restoration Action Plan results in improvement in watershed condition class. A sample of the priority watersheds will be evaluated annually to determine if they were correctly classified and if their prescribed projects could reasonably be judged to have improved actual watershed condition compared with the indicators used for classification. Ideally, completing a suite of essential projects should alter conditions in the watershed sufficiently so that if classification indicators are applied to the watershed after project completion, the watershed will rate out as being in an improved category. After a period of

time, the data from these annual evaluations can be compiled to improve program implementation. In addition, the program reviews can help to verify the rule set used to classify watershed condition classes, and they can be used to assess whether or not classes were assigned in an appropriate and consistent manner across the Forest Service.

The WO will evaluate, at a minimum, a sample of one watershed per region. We will select watersheds that were reported as having had all of the essential projects completed and reported as target accomplishments under the number of watersheds moved to an improved condition class (WTRSHD-CLS-IMP-NUM). The composition of the review team will be determined by the WO Director of the Watershed, Fish, Wildlife, Air, and Rare Plants Program Staff and includes representatives from the Watershed Condition Advisory Team, Program and Budget Analysis, and Strategic Planning and Performance Accountability Programs. Reviews may be field or office based.

Tier 2: Monitoring Watershed and Aquatic Habitat Conditions

Our long-term goal needs to be a comprehensive monitoring approach that verifies the hypothesis that concentrating activities in priority watersheds results in demonstrated improvement to stream and aquatic habitat conditions. In the context of performance accountability, we need to be able to demonstrate that the outcome of improved watershed condition actually happens on the ground and in stream channels. Establishing these linkages between upland watershed condition and instream aquatic habitat improvement has long been recognized as a significant challenge in the watershed and aquatic sciences.

In theory, watersheds that are Class 1, functioning properly, are expected to have better stream conditions than watersheds that are Class 3, functioning impaired. We can use a variety of sampling designs to verify this hypothesis, but we will not recommend a specific design at this time. Watersheds that we select to monitor in detail would have to be stratified by watershed condition class. We would then monitor stream habitat and biota at the outlet of the watersheds to see if stream conditions correlate with condition classes. Opportunities may arise by organizing the monitoring at a broad scale, such as Forest Service regions or national forests. Opportunities exist to use probability-based designs such as PACFISH/INFISH Biological Opinion (PIBO) Effectiveness Monitoring Program (Kershner et al. 2004) and Northwest Forest Plan Monitoring (Gallo et al. 2005, Reeves et al. 2004), or to take advantage of Forest Service aquatic status and trend monitoring approaches such as Aquatic Ecological Unit Inventory. Our goal is to have a comprehensive monitoring effort in place within 5 years.

We would integrate the monitoring strategy into the agency's overall watershed and aquatic evaluation program and use it in an adaptive management feedback loop to modify the approach as necessary.

Literature Cited

Bailey, R.G. 1995. Description of the ecoregions of the United States. 2nd ed., rev. Misc. Publ. No. 1391. Washington, DC: U.S. Department of Agriculture, Forest Service.

Bohn, B.A.; Kershner, J.L. 2002. Establishing aquatic restoration priorities using a watershed approach. Journal of Environmental Management. 64: 355–363.

Calkin, D.E.; Hyde, K.D.; Robichaud, P.R. et al. 2007. Assessing post-fire values-at-risk with a new calculation tool. Gen. Tech. Rep. RMRS-GTR-205. Fort Collins, CO: U.S. Department of Agriculture, Forest Service, Rocky Mountain Research Station. 32 p.

Gallo, K.; Lanigan, S.H.; Eldred, P. et al. 2005. Northwest forest plan—the first 10 years (1994–2003): preliminary assessment of the condition of watersheds. Gen. Tech. Rep. PNW-GTR-647. Portland, OR: U.S. Department of Agriculture, Forest Service, Pacific Northwest Research Station. 133 p.

Heller, D. 2004. A paradigm shift in watershed restoration. Forum for Research and Extension in Natural Resources (FOREX), Streamline Watershed Management Bulletin. 8(1): 21–23.

Karr, J.R.; Chu, L.W. 1999. Restoring life in running rivers: better biological monitoring. Washington, DC: Island Press. 206 p.

Kershner, J.L.; Archer, E.K.; Coles-Ritchie, M. et al. 2004. Guide to effective monitoring of aquatic and riparian resources. Gen. Tech. Rep. RMRS-GTR-121. U.S. Department of Agriculture, Forest Service, Fort Collins, CO.

Lackey, R.T. 2001. Values, policy, and ecosystem health. Bioscience. 51: 437–443.

McCammon, B.J.; Rector, J.; and Gebhardt, K. 1998. A framework for analyzing the hydrologic condition of watersheds. BLM Tech. Note 405, BLM/RS/ST-98/004+7210. 48 p.

National Research Council. 1999. New strategies for America's watersheds. Washington, DC: National Academy Press, Committee on Watershed Management.

Newbold, S.C. 2002. Integrated modeling for watershed management: multiple objectives and spatial effects. Journal of the American Water Resources Association. 38(2): 341–353.

Office of Management and Budget (OMB). 2006. Forest Service watershed program assessment. Washington, DC: Office of Management and Budget. http://www.whitehouse.gov/omb/expectmore/summary/10003029.2006.html. (4 August 2010).

Ogg, C.W.; Keith, G.A. 2002. New Federal support for priority watershed management needs. Journal of the American Water Resources Association. 38(2): 577–586.

Reeves, G.H.; Hohler, D.B.; Larsen, D.P. et al. 2004. Effectiveness monitoring for the aquatic and riparian component of the Northwest forest plan: conceptual framework and options. Gen. Tech. Rep. PNW-GTR-577. Portland, OR: U.S. Department of Agriculture, Forest Service, Pacific Northwest Research Station.

Regier, H.A. 1993. The notion of natural and cultural integrity. In: Woodley, S.J.; Kay, J.J.; Francis, G. Ecological integrity and the management of ecosystems. Delray Beach, FL: St. Lucie Press: 3–18.

Regional Ecosystem Office, Regional Interagency Executive Committee. 1995. Ecosystem analysis at the watershed scale: the Federal guide for watershed analysis. Sections I and II, Version 2.2. Portland, OR: U.S. Department of Agriculture, Forest Service, Pacific Northwest Region.

Reid, L.M.; Ziemer, R.R.; Furniss, M.J. 1996. Watershed analysis on Federal lands of the Pacific Northwest. Humboldt Interagency Watershed Analysis Center Workshop, McKinleyville, CA. http://www.fs.fed.us/psw/rsl/projects/water/1WhatisWA.htm. (23 August 2010).

Rosgen, D.L. 2006. Watershed assessment of river stability and sediment supply (WARSSS). Fort Collins, CO: Wildland Hydrology Books. www.epa.gov/warsss. (24 August 2010).

Sedell, J.; Sharpe, M.; Apple, D.D. et al. 2000. Water and the Forest Service. FS-660. Washington, DC: U.S. Department of Agriculture, Forest Service.

Smith, R.D.; Klimas, C.V.; Kleiss, B.A. 2005. A watershed assessment tool for evaluating ecological condition, proposed impacts, and restoration potential at multiple scales. SWWRP Technical Notes Collection, ERDC TNSWWRP-05-3. Vicksburg, MS: U.S. Army Engineer Research and Development Center.

Suter, G.W. 1993. Critique of ecosystem health concepts and indexes. Environmental Toxicology and Chemistry. 12: 1533–1539.

U.S. Department of Agriculture (USDA). 2010. Strategic plan FY 2010–2015. Washington, DC: U.S. Department of Agriculture. 50 p. http://www.ocfo.usda.gov/usdasp/sp2010/sp2010.pdf. (4 August 2010).

U.S. Department of Agriculture (USDA) Forest Service. 2011. Forest Service watershed condition classification technical guide. Washington, DC: U.S. Department of Agriculture, Forest Service, Watershed, Fish, Wildlife, Air, and Rare Plants Program.

U.S. Department of Agriculture (USDA) Forest Service. 2004a. Watershed protection and management. Forest Service Manual 2520. Washington, DC: U.S. Department of Agriculture, Forest Service. 44 p.

U.S. Department of Agriculture (USDA) Forest Service. 2004b. USDA Forest Service strategic plan for fiscal years 2004–2008. FS-810. Washington, DC: U.S. Department of Agriculture, Forest Service. 32 p.

U.S. Department of Agriculture (USDA) Forest Service. 2007. USDA Forest Service strategic plan for fiscal years 2007–2012. FS-880. Washington, DC: U.S. Department of Agriculture, Forest Service. 32 p.

U.S. Department of Agriculture (USDA) Forest Service. 2009. FY 2009 final program direction, chapter 14 National Forest Systems. Managing for Results Web page. http://fsweb.wo.fs.fed.us/results/xfst/local-resources/scripts/pullContent.php?directory=/results/pdb/Program%20Direction/FY%202009/&pagename=FY09%20Program%20Direction&category=budget&icon=budget. (14 March 2011).

U.S. Department of Agriculture (USDA) Forest Service. 2010. FY 2011 President's budget justification. Managing for Results Web page. http://www.fs.fed.us/publications/budget-2011/fy-2011-usfs-budget-justification.pdf. (14 March 2011).

U.S. Department of Agriculture (USDA) Forest Service. 2011. FY 2011 final program direction, chapter 14 National Forest Systems. Managing for Results Web page. http://fsweb.wo.fs.fed.us/results/xfst/local-resources/scripts/pullContent.php?directory=/results/pdb/Program%20Direction/FY%202011/&pagename=FY11%20Program%20Direction&category=budget&icon=budget. (14 March 2011).

Williams, J.E.; Wood, C.A.; Dombeck, M.P. (eds). 1997. Watershed restoration: principles and practices. Bethesda, MD: American Fisheries Society: 80–95.

Yount, J.D.; Niemi, G.J. 1990. Recovery of lotic communities and ecosystems from disturbance—a narrative case study. Environmental Management. 14: 547–570.

Ziemer, R.R. 1997. Temporal and spatial scales. In: Williams, J.E.; Wood, C.A.; Dombeck, M.P. Watershed restoration: principles and practices. Bethesda, MD: American Fisheries Society: 80–95.